Ancient Egyptians

WOMEN
IN
HISTORY

ANCIENT EGYPT

FIONA MACDONALD

Chrysalis Children's Books

This edition published in 2003 by

Ɛ Chrysalis Children's Books

The Chrysalis Building, Bramley Rd, London W10 6SP

ISBN 1 84138 881 5

British Library Cataloguing in Publication Data for this book is available from the British Library.

Series editor: Claire Edwards
Series designer: Jamie Asher
Cover designer: Keren-Orr Greenfeld
Picture researcher: Diana Morris
Consultant: Nicole Douek

Printed in Hong Kong
10 9 8 7 6 5 4 3 2 1

Picture acknowledgements:
Aegyptisches Museum Berlin: /AKG London 32t /C M Dixon front cover br, 33b /Werner Forman Archive 31t.
AKG London: 33t. Anthropological Museum, Turin: /E T Archive 24bl. Bonhams, London: /Bridgeman Art Library 16 l. Bridgeman Art Library/Giraudon: 3r, 31b.
By courtesy of the Trustees of the British Museum, London: 12b, 15b, 21t, 39t /AKG London 30b/ C M Dixon 43b /Werner Forman Archive 3cr, 16b, 18, 35b.

Picture acknowledgements cont…
Brooklyn Museum of Art, New York: /Bridgeman Art Library:10b. Bernard Cox/Bridgeman Art Library: 39b.
C M Dixon: 3cl, 4t, 7t, 7b, 15t, 17b, 34, 41t, 42bl.
Egyptian Museum, Cairo: /BAL/Giraudon 35t/ E T Archive front cover cl, 8t,11b/ Werner Forman Archive 12t, 19b, 28b, 40, 45 l /Jürgen Liepe Photo-Archiv 27b. Fitzwilliam Museum, Cambridge: /Bridgeman Art Library: 25t, 44 l.
Freud Museum, London: /Bridgeman Art Library: 26b.
Werner Forman Archive: 1, 32b, 38, 41b, 43t.
Kunsthistorisches Wien: /AKG London-Erich Lessing: 24br.
Iraq Museum, Bagdad: /AKG London- Erich Lessing:14.
Erich Lessing/AKG London: front cover bl, 3 l, 3c, 4b, 5b, 11t, 19t, 20b, 22b, 23t, 23b. Liepzig Museum: /Jürgen Liepe Photo-Archiv 21b. Musée des Beaux Arts, Grenoble: /Bridgeman Art Library: 36. Musée du Louvre: /AKG London-Erich Lessing 13b, 23 /Bridgeman Art Library back cover b, 20t, 29t /E T Archive 29b. Musées Royaux du Cinquantenaire,Brussels: /Werner Forman Archive: 8b.
National Archaeological Museum, Florence: /C M Dixon: 37b. Oriental Museum, Durham University: /Bridgeman Art Library: 28t, 44r. Private Collection/Werner Forman Archive: 17t. Royal Albert Memorial Museum, Exeter: /Bridgeman Art Library 42r. Science Photo Library: 9b.
Jürgen Sorges/AKG London: back cover t, 37t.
Dr E. Stoudhal/Werner Forman Archive: 6b. Rockefeller Museum, Israel: /AKG London-Erich Lessing 44 r.
University College, London: /Werner Forman Archive: 26t.

Quotations on pp 8, 11 [first view], 13, 14, 15, 16, 36 & 42 from WOMEN IN ANCIENT EGYPT, by Gay Robins, © British Museum, British Museum Press.

211 words (pp 6, 10, 11 [second view], 24, 34 & 35 [both]) from DAUGHTERS OF ISIS, WOMEN IN ANCIENT EGYPT by Joyce Tyldesley, Penguin Books (1994), © Joyce Tyldesley (1994).

66 words (p39) from HATCHEPSUT, THE FEMALE PHARAOH by Joyce Tyldesley, Penguin Books (1996), © Joyce Tyldesley (1996).

CONTENTS

The kingdom on the Nile

Egyptian civilization began more than 8000 years ago, when farmers living on the banks of the River Nile in North Africa discovered how to plant wheat and barley. By 5000 BC they had learned how to domesticate sheep, goats and cattle, and by 3500 BC they were living in villages built of mud bricks. By about 3100 BC northern and southern Egypt were united as one nation. The kingdom of ancient Egypt survived for the next 3000 years.

Farming by the Nile

Most of Egypt is desert. The ancient Egyptians called it the Red Land, and no one could live there. But every year the River Nile flooded its banks, spreading a layer of sticky black mud on either side. This created rich, fertile soil, which the Egyptians called the Black Land. Here crops of wheat, barley, fruit and vegetables grew rapidly in the hot summer sun. The Egyptians believed that their land had been blessed by the gods.

For most of its long history Egypt was ruled by men. This wall-painting shows Pharaoh Amenhotep I, who reigned from 1525 to 1504 BC. His false beard is a sign of male royal power.

Monuments and jewels

In cities and towns Egyptian craftsmen made jewellery from gold and precious stones, mined in the desert or offered as tribute. Some metals, such as silver, were brought from nearby lands. Egyptian builders constructed pyramids, temples, palaces and tombs, and craftsmen created beautiful carvings, wall paintings and statues. Neighbouring nations envied the Egyptian people and their splendid civilization.

This wall-painting shows Egyptian farmers threshing wheat. Men also caught fish and waterfowl from the river. Egyptian men and women harvested flax from the river banks to spin and weave into fine linen cloth.

4

Egypt grew up along the banks of the Nile. Most palaces and temples were built on the east bank, the land of the living, where the sun rises. Most tombs were built on the west bank, the land of the dead, where the sun sets.

Map labels:
Mediterranean Sea
Delta
Giza
Memphis
Saqqara
Desert
The Nile
El-Amarna
Red Sea
Valley of the Kings
Karnak
Thebes
Nubia

ANCIENT EGYPT TIME LINE

Pre-dynastic 5500–3100 BC
First farming villages built. Increasing contacts between peoples of upper (southern) and lower (northern) Egypt.

Early dynastic 3100–2686 BC
Kingdom of Egypt formed c. 3100 BC when Egypt was united under one ruler, called the pharaoh.

Old Kingdom 2686–2181 BC
An age of strong pharaohs and pyramid building.

First Intermediate Period 2181–2055 BC
Time of troubles. Egypt divided. Weak kings rule.

Middle Kingdom 2055–1650 BC
Powerful pharaohs rule. Nubia (south of Egypt) conquered, new lands farmed. Many works of art.

Second Intermediate Period 1650–1550 BC
Foreign kings from the Middle East rule Egypt.

New Kingdom 1550–1069 BC
Egyptian pharaohs rule. Creation of great empire. Trade expands to African and Mediterranean lands. Many fine works of art, including Tutankhamun's tomb. New capital city at Thebes.

Third Intermediate Period 1069–747 BC
Egypt divided. Kings from Nubia rule southern Egypt.

Late Period 747–332 BC
Egypt's power weakens. In 525 BC Egypt conquered by Persia.

Ptolemaic Period 332–30 BC
King Alexander the Great of Macedon (north of Greece) invades. Egypt ruled by Greek kings (and queens, including Cleopatra).

Roman Period 30 BC–395 AD
Egypt conquered by Rome, and becomes part of the Roman Empire.

The Egyptians lived in the narrow strip of fertile land between the river and the mountains and desert.

Tombs, temples and treasures

Many wonderful treasures have survived from ancient Egyptian times. How much do they tell us about Egyptian women's lives?

Art with a meaning

All Egyptian art had a purpose. Palaces were homes for mighty rulers, temples were houses for the gods. Statues were monuments to a pharaoh's power and achievements, jewellery displayed the wearer's wealth and taste. Tombs, tomb paintings and lovely objects buried alongside bodies were meant to help dead people enjoy life in the next world. Because of this, Egyptian art was not designed to give accurate portraits of men or women, or to reflect real life. Instead, it showed Egyptian people as they would like to be seen, alive or after death. It also presented a powerful message about Egypt's splendid civilization to the world outside.

A group of pyramids at Giza. The largest, the Great Pyramid, was built for Pharaoh Khufu, who died in about 2528 BC. The pyramid was supposed to protect the pharaoh while his spirit travelled through the world of the dead on its way to meet the gods.

> *She who once lacked even a box now has furniture, while she who used to see her face in the water now owns a mirror.*
>
> COMMENT BY A MIDDLE KINGDOM SCRIBE ON THE WEALTH OF EGYPT

Mostly for men

But Egyptian art did reflect real life in some important ways. It tells us that Egyptian men and women were fond of looking at beautiful buildings, carvings and paintings, and of wearing elegant jewels, wigs and clothes. It also tells us about the differences in power and influence between Egyptian women and men. Because men were the richest and most powerful people in Egyptian society, most buildings, paintings and treasures were created for men and portrayed mainly men. When women did appear in Egyptian art, they were often shown in the background, as companions and helpers. Sometimes they were shown smaller than men too.

Painted papyrus showing the scribe Ani, who lived around 1200 BC, playing draughts. His wife sits behind him. This was a common way of showing husbands and wives in paintings. In real life, husbands and wives probably sat side by side.

Men's world, women's world

In paintings and sculptures women were almost always shown with pale-coloured skins, while men were shown suntanned. Historians think that this is because women spent much of their time indoors, in a female world apart from men. Unlike men, they did not get suntanned by working in the hot sunshine on building sites, in the army or in the fields. Sometimes, to pass on a special message to the viewer, women might be painted black, the colour of the fertile Egyptian soil, or even green, the colour of life and rebirth. This tells us that women were valued not only for themselves, but also for the children they produced.

An ideal image

Women in the foreground of paintings and carvings were almost all shown as young, slim and beautiful, whatever they looked like in real life. This partly reflected fashions and ideas about women's attractiveness, but some historians think that it also showed women's weakness compared with men. Rich, powerful Egyptian men liked to be pictured as strong and well-built, or even fat. That showed they could afford lots of food to eat.

This gold and turquoise pectoral (an ornament worn on the chest) is decorated with the figure of a winged goddess. She is shown as young, slim and beautiful.

Hidden from history

The Egyptians were one of the first people to invent a system of writing. In fact, they had three different kinds: hieroglyphs, for formal inscriptions, hieratic for writing on papyrus paper, and, later, demotic for quick, scribbled notes.

As far as we know, all written records were created by men. Most surviving documents and inscriptions record either events and professional activities practised by men, or else show the Egyptian world seen from a man's point of view. Even popular love songs, supposedly by women, were probably written by men.

Works of art, like this portrait of Queen Meritamen, tell us what women in ancient Egypt might have looked like.

If you want to make friendship last in a house you enter, whether as lord, or brother, or friend, in any place you enter, beware of approaching the women!

FROM INSTRUCTIONS OF SCRIBE PTAHHOTEP, OLD KINGDOM

No women scribes?

Egyptian written records were produced by craftworkers, who carved inscriptions in stone and painted them on walls, and by scribes, who wrote down royal commands, business records, religious texts and law reports on papyrus and leather scrolls. They also wrote medical texts, letters, myths and legends, poems and stories. Training to be a scribe took many years and was only open to boys. We know of only five women scribes in more than 3000 years of Egyptian history.

A page from an Egyptian Book of the Dead (a guide to the afterlife). Women could not read books like these, but they may have learned a great deal by listening and remembering.

Notes and scribbles

Less important messages were scratched on bits of stone or broken pottery (called ostraca). It seems likely that these notes were also produced by men, but we cannot be sure, since few of them are signed. We do not know how many Egyptian women could read or write, even at a simple level, but it was probably only women of high society, such as princesses, businesswomen, rich families' household managers, or the wives and daughters of scribes.

Investigating women

Women do appear in many Egyptian documents and inscriptions, but the male bias in reading and writing makes it hard to find out about women's point of view. It also makes it difficult, although not impossible, to investigate many details of women's daily lives, and to discover women's beliefs, thoughts and feelings. The only written records that deal specifically with women's needs are medical scrolls, which suggest treatments for diseases. But from documents such as law reports, marriage and divorce agreements and popular stories, we can sometimes read between the lines to find out about women's lives. When the study of these documents is combined with the latest scientific techniques, a picture of Egyptian women slowly takes shape.

Truth or guesswork

Historians and archaeologists have studied ancient Egyptian civilization for more than 200 years. They have made fascinating discoveries, but there are still many things about ancient Egypt that they do not know. Some of the statements in this book are based on possible interpretations of difficult or partly-missing evidence. Others tell the truth as historians understand it today. But history never stops, and there may be many exciting discoveries in future years that will give us an even clearer picture of ancient Egyptian life.

Scientists can find out about the health and appearance of ancient Egyptian women by investigating mummified bodies. They can also use X-rays and other techniques to make lifelike reconstructions of people who lived long ago.

WOMEN AND FAMILIES

Women's rights

People living in countries near Egypt reported that Egyptian women had more legal rights than in many other lands. There is no surviving list of ancient Egyptian laws, but by piecing together little bits of information from many different documents, historians have found out that this was true. Egyptian women were treated as equals with men in many aspects of their lives.

> *I am a free woman of Egypt. I have raised eight children, and have provided them with everything suitable to their station in life.*
>
> FROM THE WILL OF LADY NAUNAKHTE

Property-owners

Before about 500 BC the Egyptians did not use money. Instead their wealth came from owning land, animals, furniture, jewels and other goods. Women could own property, buy more or sell it if they chose. They did not need their husband's permission to do this, and they did not have to consult him when making a will. Women could leave their property to whoever they wished – sons, daughters, relatives or friends. Unlike many other countries at that time, there were no laws saying that everything had to be left to the eldest son or divided equally among all children. A wife was also allowed a share of her husband's property, and had the right to inherit some of it after his death.

This painting shows Tjepu, a rich woman who lived in the city of Thebes in about 1350 BC. All Egyptian women, rich and poor, could own property, from jewels to cooking pots.

Egyptian women often spent their leisure time in the company of men. Here a couple listen to a singer accompanying himself on a harp.

Businesswomen

Egyptian women could also work outside the home, either in their own business, or for somebody else. They could even buy their own house or have one built, if they were rich enough, without having to have a male relation as a legal guardian to protect them.

Appearing in court

If Egyptian women had serious arguments to settle, they were allowed to take legal action, by arguing a case in court. They could also be tried, in the same way as men, when they were accused of a crime. Their judgement and understanding was rated as highly as men's. Where it was appropriate, women witnesses might be called to give evidence in court. All this was dramatically different from women's legal status in many other lands, such as ancient Greece, Rome and Babylon, where even wealthy women had no right to take legal action or to speak in court.

TWO VIEWS OF WOMEN

[I married you] when I was a young man. I was with you when I was carrying out all sorts of official jobs. I was with you and I did not divorce you. I did not cause your heart to grieve. I did it ... saying 'She has always been with me'...
(LETTER FROM A HUSBAND TO HIS DEAD WIFE.)

Let your wife see your wealth but do not trust her with it... Do not open your heart to your wife, as what you say in private will be repeated in the street...
(ADVICE FROM THE SCRIBE ANHSHESHONQ)

Which of the two ancient Egyptian comments above gives us a more accurate view of relations between Egyptian women and men? Did husbands love and trust their wives, or were they scornful and suspicious? Like today, this must have varied from person to person, but these comments tell us that at least some men respected women as partners.

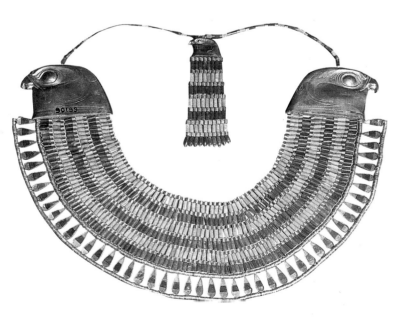

This collar was made for a princess, probably by slaves. Ordinary women could choose clay beads from a craftshop. In exchange they might offer linen, food, woven or other goods.

Husbands and wives

Ancient Egyptians were strong believers in family life. Poems and songs tell us that they hoped for a happy marriage and lots of children. They also relied on family members to help them farm their lands, run their households, and support them when times were hard.

Wedding days

The ancient Egyptians had no legal marriage ceremony. They saw marriage as a private affair, although parents might ask a scribe to draw up a formal marriage contract. There was probably a big feast to celebrate the wedding and announce it to the community. The bridegroom gave his new wife a gift (maybe even a slave, if he could afford it) and her family gave the new couple presents of household goods and food.

This jewelled gold panel from Pharaoh Tutankhamun's throne shows Queen Ankhesenamun gently and lovingly spreading perfumed oil on her husband's chest.

Unlike many civilizations, Egyptian husbands and wives spent leisure time together. This painting shows a family on a hunting expedition in the world of the dead.

Marrying young

Almost all Egyptian women married, usually in their early teens. In law, a woman could choose her own husband – even a foreigner if she liked – but most marriages were probably arranged by a girl's parents. Parents may have chosen a husband for their daughter because of his wealth. Sometimes they chose a distant relative. This helped keep family property together, and parents may have had more trust in a relative than in an unknown young man.

More than one wife

Not everything was equal in marriage. Egyptian husbands could have more than one wife, but wives could not have several husbands. In fact very few men could afford more than one wife, apart from the pharaoh, who had hundreds. (Pharaohs sometimes married for political reasons, to win the friendship of powerful rulers.) Women were expected to stay faithful to their husbands. The punishment for breaking this rule was death. In contrast, men did have affairs outside marriage, but the community strongly disapproved of any relationship with another man's wife.

Death and divorce

Divorce was possible and, like marriage, was usually arranged by families. Women also had the same rights as men to ask the courts to legally end a marriage. But most marriages were ended by death. As mummified bodies show, few Egyptians lived much longer than 40 years. Women died in childbirth, men died from accidents or in wars, and both were killed by diseases such as polio and leprosy.

For the Egyptians, a happy marriage meant having children. This limestone carving shows the royal supervisor Djehontyhetep, who lived around 1560 BC, and his wife, daughter and son. As a sign of affection, they are clasping one another around the waist.

AN EGYPTIAN MARRIAGE

Padiaset arranged for Horwedja ... to be made a priest of Amun... and he gave him Nitemat, his daughter, as a wife.

The story of this marriage was first written down in about 600 BC. Horwedja (a young priest) visited Padiaset (an older priest) at his house. He saw Padiaset's daughter, Nitemat, and wanted to marry her. Padiaset told Horwedja to wait a year, because Nitemat was too young, but meanwhile helped him to make progress in his career. This story tells us what the two men wanted, but we do not know what Nitemat, the young girl, thought or felt. Did she fall in love with the young priest, or did she just obey her father's wishes? The ancient Egyptian scribe did not think it worthwhile to record her views.

Children

Children were one of the main purposes of marriage. Fertility dolls were often buried alongside people in tombs, so that they would have many children in the life after death. Medical texts had recipes for drugs to help women become pregnant. Women with many children were seen as successful and attractive. Sons were especially valued, because they could support their parents in old age. It was also important to have a son or daughter at your funeral to make sure you lived again in the afterlife.

Dangerous times

Even though children were welcomed, pregnancy and childbirth were the most dangerous times of a woman's life. Babyhood was risky, too. One in five babies and children may have died from fevers or disease. Egyptian women tried to protect themselves and their children with amulets, prayers and lucky charms. New babies were given a name as soon as they were born. Without one, they could not survive when they passed into the world of the dead.

Baby care

Mothers from ordinary families cared for and nursed their own children, often breastfeeding them until they were three years old. Women from rich families employed professional wet-nurses instead. They also paid for expert midwives to attend them while giving birth. Ordinary women relied on help from family or friends.

A bronze statue of the dwarf god Bes, who protected mothers and babies. Egyptian women made offerings to Bes, asking for his help.

Spell ... for a child, a fledgling:
Are you hot in the nest?
Are you burning in the bush?
Your mother is not with you?
There is no sister to fan you?
There is no nurse to offer protection?
Let there be brought to me a pellet of gold,
Forty beads, a cornelian seal-stone,
With a crocodile and a hand on it,
to fell, to drive off, this Demon of Desire,
to warm the limbs,
to fell these male and female enemies from the West [land of the Dead].

PART OF A MAGIC SPELL TO PROTECT A CHILD
AGAINST FEVER

This was a common scene in Egypt – a woman protectively leading a young child. Egyptian children were loved and well cared for.

Help around the house

Older girls had to help around the house and look after younger brothers and sisters. Once they were big and strong enough, boys were usually trained to follow their father's profession, perhaps as a craftsman, farmer or scribe. Boys from wealthier families might be sent to school. Girls did not go to school. For girls especially, childhood did not last long. They were usually married by the time they were 13 or 14, as soon as they were physically able to have children. Boys probably married later, when they were 20 years old, or more. Possibly this was because they waited until they had learned a special skill or were wealthier before marrying.

Looking after children

Bringing up children was always women's work. Ordinary mothers washed, cleaned and cared for their children. Rich or royal boys sometimes had male tutors to teach them reading and writing, but were looked after by women servants and slaves. Mothers gave their children simple toys, such as wooden balls and little clay animals, to play with, but also trained their daughters to help with women's work, such as cooking or weaving cloth. From an early age, boys and girls played separately, and did not join in one another's tasks and activities.

Egyptian children liked playing with dolls, balls, rattles, spinning tops and model animals. This toy lion was made of wood with metal teeth. When the string was pulled, its jaws snapped shut.

15

WOMEN AT HOME

Mistress of the house

Although the law gave Egyptian women many rights, Egyptian men still regarded themselves as the head of the household. However, the Egyptians realized that running a home was a responsible task. They usually gave married women the respectful title of Mistress of the House.

Do not control your wife in her house when you know she is efficient. Do not say to her 'Where is it? Get it' when she has put something in its correct place. Let your eye observe her in silence; then you will recognise her skill, and it will be a joy...

ADVICE TO YOUNG MEN BY A NEW KINGDOM SCRIBE

This mummy-case is decorated with the name of the young woman it was made for. She died around 800 BC. Her title is 'Mistress of the House Djedmontuiuesankh, wife of Pamiu'.

The scribe Nakhte and his wife, walking in their garden in about 1500 BC. Their house is larger than many Egyptian houses, with four rooms in the upper storey and a large front doorway.

Housekeepers

As the person in charge of the household, a woman had many tasks. She had to look after the house and all its contents, and care for the people who lived there. She was in charge of sweeping, tidying and cleaning – dust and flies were a constant problem. She also had to rid her house of pests such as mice, scorpions and snakes. Even if she was too rich or noble to do hard, practical work herself, she still had to organize servants and slaves to do it for her.

An ivory carving of a woman collecting lotus flowers by the river bank. Women helped with the harvest, picked fruits such as grapes and figs, and gathered flowers.

Food, farms, families

A woman (or her servants) also had to prepare, cook and serve food. She was responsible for storing grain, and measuring it out so that it lasted all year long. When family members fell ill, she nursed them, mixed herbal medicines, said prayers and recited spells. If the illness looked serious, and the family could afford it, she might call in a doctor. In farming families, women helped care for the animals, especially at busy times such as lambing. Women also looked after the family pets. The most popular were cats, dogs and monkeys.

Monkeys were favourite pets among the royal family. This carving shows a monkey crouching under a royal woman's chair.

Surrounded by women

Apart from the pharaoh, men usually had only one wife. Yet Egyptian households were often large, and contained many women. As well as the family unit of mother, father and children, a household might also include relatives, such as grandmothers and aunts, servants and slaves. Living and working side by side with other females – and giving orders to some of them – was a normal part of most women's lives. Compared with many people today, Egyptian women had very little privacy, but they always had someone on hand to help with chores or child care.

Working at home

In addition to all this, a woman might use part of the family house as a workshop, making items such as baskets or sandals to barter in the marketplace. Spinning thread and weaving cloth were also women's tasks. Egyptian women were expected to make enough cloth to supply their families with sleeping rugs, towels and clothes. If they had any left over, they could take it to market, to exchange for other goods they or their family needed.

Relatives, servants and slaves

When a young girl married, she left her parent's home and moved to live with her husband. But often the young couple did not set up their own household. Instead they lived with the husband's parents, at least until the husband had enough wealth to build a new home. So an Egyptian household might consist of an older married couple and several married sons, their wives and children.

> I have brought to Egypt to be slaves those whom my sword spared, as numerous captives ... also their wives and children.
>
> FROM AN INSCRIPTION MADE ON THE ORDERS OF PHARAOH RAMESES II

> I am making a will in favour of my wife... I am giving her three slaves from Asia, which my brother ... Ankhreni gave to me.
>
> FROM A WILL MADE BY A SCRIBE

Women without men

Unmarried daughters also lived at home with their parents, along with other female relations. Although young widows usually remarried, an elderly widow, or a widow who was sickly, might not be able to find a new husband. These women could live alone if they wanted to. But Egyptians liked the close companionship of families and saw it as a normal way of life. It was also difficult, though not impossible, for a single woman (widowed or unmarried) from an ordinary family to support herself.

A tomb model of a woman servant made in about 2500 BC. She is carrying a basket of loaves and meat on her head.

Servants

Wealthy Egyptian families employed male and female servants to help run the household. Servants came from Egyptian families who did not have enough land or other work to support all their members. Usually, they lived in their employer's home. Wealthy families built special blocks of servants quarters, away from the main house. Women servants worked at typically female tasks, such as baby care, cooking and serving food, brewing, grinding corn, baking bread, spinning and weaving. They also worked as personal maids to wealthy women, helping them bathe and put on jewellery, arranging their hair and their wigs, and looking after their clothes.

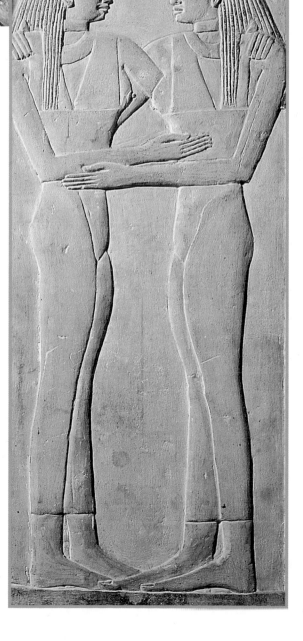

Ordinary women sometimes worked as personal maids to wealthy women, helping them dress and putting on their make-up.

Slaves

Slaves were usually captured in wars. Egyptian men (and their wives and children) might also be enslaved as a punishment for serious crimes, or volunteer to become slaves to pay off their debts. Women could own slaves, just like any other property. There are also a few examples of women slave-owners who hired out slaves to other people at daily rates of pay. Women slaves worked at the same tasks as female servants, spinning and weaving large amounts of cloth. Slaves were valuable, and usually well-treated. They could own property, and save up to buy their own freedom. Some women slaves married their male owners, and others were given their freedom.

Living with other women, especially female relatives, was a part of everyday life. This limestone carving shows a warm embrace between Ihat, wife of the scribe Nikaure, on the left, and her mother Hetepheres.

19

Living in workmen's villages

There is little evidence about ordinary people's homes. Their houses and unmarked graves have mostly disappeared. But archaeologists have discovered two sites, called Deir el-Medina and Tell el-Amarna, that reveal many details of ancient

Workers' homes

Deir el-Medina was built to house workmen building the pharaohs' tombs, and their families, from around 1550 to 1069 BC. It is not entirely typical of the rest of Egypt, but gives us the best evidence we have of ordinary people's lives. The city of Tell el-Amarna was built as a new capital for Pharaoh Akhenaten between 1352 and 1336 BC. One area of the city seems to have been set apart for workmen and their families. Another area, closer to the royal palace, was where the scribes and administrators lived.

The desert ruins of the village Deir el-Medina, near Thebes. About 120 Egyptian families lived here in houses built of sun-dried mud bricks.

Women stored food and other goods in baskets like these, woven from palm leaves. They have been preserved by Egypt's dry desert environment for more than 3000 years.

A crowded street

From these sites, we can learn about the layout of ordinary Egyptian homes. At Tell el-Amarna the workers' houses were crowded together side by side, facing endways on to the street. They were only about 10 metres long and 5 metres wide. Inside, each house was divided into three rooms. The room nearest the street was used to house animals, or as a food-preparation area and craft workshop.

This pillar (called a votive stele) was built as an offering to a god. It shows a workman and his wife kneeling together with hands raised in prayer. Only the wealthiest workers could afford to pay for works of art such as this.

Sitting and sleeping

The living room was the largest room in the house, measuring about 5 metres square. A low ledge, used for sitting and sleeping, ran around two sides of this room. Most people sat on mats on the floor, or on low stools. Big jars of drinking water were also kept here, and it was a woman's job to fetch water from the river or well. There were spaces high up in the walls to hold oil lamps. A third room was divided into two. One part was used as a bedroom, the other for storage and cooking. A staircase led up to the flat roof, which was used as extra space for working, sitting and sleeping. At Deir el-Medina, the houses were bigger. Many had cellars, more space for cooking, and extra bedrooms. Unlike men, who worked outside the home, most women spent nearly all their lives in surroundings like these.

Community life

Many records from the law courts have survived from Deir el-Medina, together with notes and sketches on pottery fragments, called ostraca. They tell us that women played an active part in community life. There were a few women traders and property owners. Women appeared before the court accused of theft, non-payment of debts, selling property they didn't own, and not caring for sick relatives. There were divorce cases in which women stood up for their rights and even mocked their husbands.

Women's notes

Some of the ostraca, written in hieroglyphs, suggest that a few women might have known how to read and write. They cover topics such as laundry lists, and notes on dressmaking and underwear. There are also drawings of women with newborn babies. Historians think that these may have been a form of magic, creating imaginary safe places where babies could be born.

Pots were used for many everyday activities, such as carrying water or storing grain. Simple pots were shaped from mud. Better quality pots, like these, were made from fine clay.

WOMEN AND WORK

Household managers

Egyptian women spent most of their time at home. But they were still very busy. As well as running their own homes, women also worked at a number of different jobs that used their domestic skills and knowledge.

Keepers of the dining hall

When wealthy and powerful women died, their titles and achievements were usually listed on their tombs. From this evidence we know that a few women from upper-class families were employed by leading nobles as household managers in their homes and palaces. They supervised the servants who cooked and cleaned, who served food and drink at table, and who welcomed guests. One woman was described as the keeper of the dining hall – a very important job. Women were also often put in charge of organizing and controlling the supplies of food and drink in these noble homes.

Managing workshops

Some women worked as overseers of workshops on noblemen's estates. These were usually weaving rooms for making wigs and clothes. Almost always, women supervised groups of other women workers. It was unusual for women to give orders to groups of men. Households headed by a woman – a powerful priestess, for example, or a widowed noblewoman – were often managed and run by female staff.

Women often worked in garden plots, or helped their husband in the fields close to home. This painting shows a husband and wife ploughing.

Servant girls offering food and drink to a seated woman at a feast. On these occasions women mixed freely with men, laughing and talking.

Honest and trustworthy

On tomb memorials, women are sometimes described as sealers. These were people who fastened treasury or food-store doors with a seal, to keep the valuable contents safe. The ancient Egyptians did not have locks with keys, so doors were sealed with a small lump of mud. Once a door had been sealed shut, it could only be opened by breaking the seal. Being a sealer was a very responsible job. Unlike some other ancient civilizations, the Egyptians believed that women could be trusted just as much as men.

No training

Although a few women showed that they were capable of managing organizations and could do the work of their husbands when they were absent or ill, they never worked at the top public jobs in Egyptian society. They could not be viziers, army commanders or administrators. There was no law banning women from these posts, but they could not read and write, and had no chance of making contacts at court. Also, they could not train to be scribes, which was an essential qualification for most government jobs.

Serving maids and entertainers

Women could go out to work as cooks, servants, singers and dancers. The ancient Egyptians were fond of music, and groups of women musicians and dancers were very popular as entertainers at feasts. Talented performers were richly rewarded and earned great respect. There may have been families of professional musicians who made careers as entertainers for many generations.

Women musicians, around 1450 BC. They are playing, from left to right, a harp, a lute and a lyre.

Food and drink

Normally Egyptian families ate one main meal a day, at lunchtime, while they sheltered indoors from the noonday sun. They had small snacks at breakfast and supper time. On special occasions, wealthy people held feasts in the evening as well.

MENU FOR AN EGYPTIAN BANQUET
Bread, barley porridge, fish, pigeon stew, kidneys, roast beef, figs, berries, honey cakes, cheese, wine.

FOOD BURIED IN A WEALTHY WOMAN'S TOMB, TO NOURISH HER SPIRIT IN THE WORLD OF THE DEAD

Hard work

The Egyptians had no way of keeping food cool, so each meal had to be freshly-prepared. Cooking was women's work. Wives, daughters, women servants and slaves spent a large amount of time every day preparing food. Cooking was hard, tiring work. Women had only simple tools to prepare food, and had to fetch water – usually from the River Nile – to boil meat, fish and vegetables. They collected straw and animal dung to light fires and heat ovens.

Daily bread

Bread and beer were the two most important items in the Egyptian diet. Bread was made from grain, ground on stone to make flour. This was mixed with water, shaped into round, flat loaves, then baked in a clay oven. Sometimes yeast was added to make light, spongy loaves, but only wealthy families could afford this. Ordinary people ate large amounts of bread. The pharaoh's workmen were given food wages of ten loaves a day for each man. Egyptian women had to bake fresh bread every day because loaves quickly went stale and dry.

TOOTHACHE

Egyptian bread was very coarse. It often contained particles of stone left by grinding the grain to make flour, or sand blown in from the desert. As a result, most Egyptian people's teeth became chipped or worn, as you can see from these teeth, taken from an Egyptian mummy. People also suffered from gum infections, which would have given them terrible toothache.

A woman servant grinding corn. She is crushing the grains against a stone slab using a stone roller.

A tomb model, made from wood, clay and linen, showing women servants making bread and brewing beer. They are working to mix flour and water, and to knead the bread dough. Many women spent their lives working together in groups like this.

Barley beer

Women made beer by mixing part-baked loaves of barley with water in big pottery jars, and leaving the mixture to stand in a warm place to ferment. Sometimes they added dates, honey or spices. After several days the beer became fizzy, but it was so thick that it had to be sieved, or sucked up through a wooden tube fitted with a strainer. Egyptian beer was not very alcoholic. In fact it was often given to children because it was good for them, and they probably liked its sweet taste. Some Egyptian paintings show men harvesting grapes and making wine. But only wealthy people could afford wine.

Meat and vegetables

The Egyptians ate onions, garlic and cucumbers. They bartered for these at the local market or grew them in garden plots. Women may have helped to look after these plots while the men worked in the fields. Farmers also grew chickpeas, beans, lentils, grapes, figs and dates. Meat was eaten on festival days only, unless the men were good hunters, and could catch wild hare and gazelle in the desert. Most people could afford fish, fresh or salted, from the River Nile. Some families kept ducks and geese for their eggs, and bees to give honey. Women mixed honey with flour to make sweet cakes.

Grain grew well in Egypt, and surplus grain was sold to nearby countries. Here men are loading sacks of grain on board ship. Overseas trade was part of a world in which women played no part.

Cloth-making

Egyptian cloth was nearly all made of linen. There were several reasons for this. Flax, the plant linen is made from, grew well in damp fields by the river, and linen cloth was cool and comfortable to wear in Egypt's warm climate. Its fibres soaked up sweat but did not trap the dirt. It could also be washed again and again. Women weavers made fabric with 100 threads per centimetre. This is twice as fine as the best linen fabric made today.

Mass production

Linen is made from thread, spun from the stems of the flax plant. Most flax was grown on estates belonging to great families or rich temples, although families also grew it on small farms. Men planted and harvested flax, and threshed the flower-heads from the stalks, but the rest of linen production was carried out by women. Many big estates had teams of specially-trained women servants who spent all their time making cloth. They worked in big weaving rooms, almost like factories. Each group of women had one particular task, then passed what they had made on to other workers further along the production line.

This Egyptian shirt is probably the oldest surviving garment in the world. It was made around 3000 BC from fine linen cloth, and has a pleated bodice and sleeves.

Egyptian women often wove special linen bandages to wrap the bodies of the dead when they were mummified. This mummy-bandage is decorated with scenes from a Book of the Dead (a guide to the afterlife).

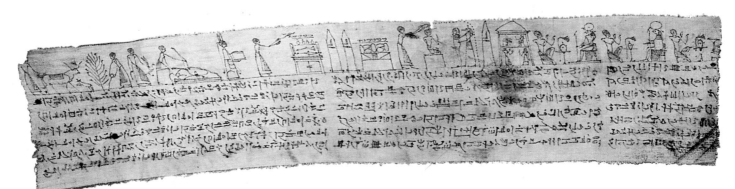

Retting, spinning and weaving

First, women had to ret the flax – this meant soaking it to remove the outer casing of each stalk and soften the long linen fibres inside. Then they joined, twisted and spun the fibres using a simple spindle. They wound the thread into hanks or balls, stretched warp threads across long horizontal looms, then finally wove the cloth. Older women acted as supervisors and they did not allow any slacking.

A weaving servant's life was very hard. Often, servants brought their children to work with them. Children would be safe in the workshop, and could learn useful skills. Boys as well as girls needed to know how to spin, since it was a man's job to spin ropes.

At home

Women working at home, alone groups, spun and wove linen in the same way as women in workshops. But they had to fit in cloth-making alongside all their other household tasks. Weaving looms were often set up on the flat roofs of Egyptian houses, since they took up a lot of space. It hardly ever rains in Egypt, so there was no danger of water damage, but thick cloth awnings were sometimes hung on poles to protect people from the hot sun.

This tomb model shows Egyptian women in a workshop weaving linen cloth on long horizontal looms.

NEW TECHNOLOGY

In the New Kingdom, in about 1500 BC, new weaving technology spread to Egypt from the Middle East. People began to make patterned tapestry cloths, woven from wool on big, upright looms. For the first time men began to work as professional weavers, making this new-style cloth. But most cloth, made from traditional linen, was still produced by women. Women also continued to use linen cloth for barter and trade. Visitors to Egypt found these male weavers and women traders remarkable. Herodotus, a Greek writer who visited Egypt in about 450 BC, wrote, 'The Egyptians do almost everything the opposite way round from other people ... the women go to market and do business, while the men stay at home and weave.'

Clothes and make-up

Today clothes send out many signals about us, such as our wealth, our age and, often, the kind of work we do. It was the same in ancient Egypt. Royal fashions changed over the centuries but, for work and for relaxing, most ordinary women continued to wear very simple clothes.

Clothes for comfort

Women usually wore long, loose linen tunics, either with or without sleeves. These were comfortable to work in, and adaptable to women's changing shape. (Most women would have been pregnant for quite a large part of their lives.) Clothes were expensive. A tunic might cost twice as much as a goat, and would be worn for many years. Worn-out robes were used to make cleaning rags, or torn into strips to make bandages for wrapping mummies. On winter evenings, women wore a warm woollen shawl. Usually men and women went barefoot, but sometimes they wore flat open sandals, made by men from reeds or leather.

This statue, made in about 1400 BC, shows a servant girl carrying a large jar. She is wearing a necklace and a decorated belt.

Almost naked

Girls under child-bearing age, slaves and servant women, often wore very few clothes. Statues and wall-paintings show them dressed in just a short wrap-around skirt, or sometimes nothing at all. This was practical – they did not need warmth or rainproof protection, and long, flowing garments would have got in the way of women's work or children's play. Unlike many ancient civilizations, the Egyptians were not embarrassed by the naked human body. But dress was often linked to status. Rich, powerful people, especially men, are usually shown wearing clothes. Until the New Kingdom, upper-class women are also shown fully clothed.

Typical men's and women's clothes in about 1000 BC. The woman is wearing a long straight robe. The man is wearing a knee-length kilt.

A sketch on a piece of stone (ostracon) painted in about 1200 BC. It shows a royal woman wearing eye make-up, lipstick and rouge.

Make-up

The Egyptians believed that thick eye make-up protected their eyes from the sun's glare, and helped prevent eye disease caused by dust and flies. The most common eyeliner, made of powdered minerals mixed with oil, probably did help kill germs and insect eggs. Bright green was the most popular colour in Old Kingdom times. In the New Kingdom people preferred glittery grey. Both men and women wore this eyeliner, but only women wore rouge to colour their cheeks, and painted their lips red. Unlike eye make-up, these cosmetics had no medical use, but were simply designed to make women more attractive.

Simple sewing

Clothes for rich women were made by specially-trained servants and slaves. Ordinary women made or bartered for clothes for their families to wear. Egyptian clothes needed very little sewing. Most were simply draped and knotted round the body, or joined down the side by seams.

Washing clothes

Men ran professional laundries by the Nile riverside, used by wealthy people, but ordinary women probably washed their own families' clothes. For washing, they either pounded the wet clothes against rocks, or used a soapy mixture made from ashes, called lye. Both methods were hard on the hands. Workers on the riverbank had to keep a lookout for crocodiles as well. Clothes were usually stored in chests, along with other fabric items, such as towels. In wealthy families, and for rich tombs, the chests were brightly-painted and inlaid with precious wood and ivory.

This wooden spoon was used for mixing make-up. It is decorated with a carving of a young girl playing a lute.

ROYAL WOMEN

Close to the pharaoh

Today the word queen is easily understood. It means either the wife of a king, or else a woman who rules a country in her own right. In ancient Egypt, there was no single word meaning queen. Instead, there were three different titles describing important, powerful women who were close to the pharaoh.

Royal wives

Each pharaoh married many different wives. All had the right to the title 'royal wife'. Some were women he chose from among wealthy courtiers, some were members of his own royal family, and others were the daughters of rulers from neighbouring lands, sent to Egypt by their fathers as a way of strengthening a friendship or ending a war. These wives and their female servants spent most of their time in women's quarters (called the ipet), close to the royal palace, where they brought up their children. Documents show that they were supported by taxes paid to the pharaoh, but they also had to work, usually by spinning and weaving cloth. Although these royal wives were well-housed and well-fed, they must occasionally have felt as if they were living in a comfortable prison. Sometimes, they became involved in palace plots and schemes.

A banquet painted in about 1500 BC. The women are wearing fine jewellery and wigs. They are being served food and drink by women servants and young girls. Royal wives in women's quarters may have enjoyed banquets like this.

Great Royal Wife

The pharaoh's chief wife was given the title Great Royal Wife, and was the most important woman in the kingdom. She was often shown side by side with the pharaoh on monuments, and in statues and wall-paintings. She ranked next to the pharaoh in political and religious importance, and had many important ceremonial duties, but little real political power. Some women, like the famous Nefertari (c.1300–1250 BC) who was the first wife of Pharaoh Rameses II, may have played an important part in politics by discussing plans and policies with the pharaoh. Only one women could be the Great Royal Wife at any one time.

Sometimes, the Mother of the King had great influence over her son. Queen Tiye, who lived from about 1410 to 1340 BC, was the mother of Pharaoh Akhenaten. She received letters from rulers asking for her help and advice, even while her son was in power.

This painting shows Queen Nefertari making an offering of milk to the gods. She was appointed Great Royal Wife by her husband Rameses II.

Queen Mother

The mother of the ruling pharaoh was given the title Mother of the King. Like the Great Royal Wife she had religious and ceremonial duties, but as mother of the pharaoh, people believed she was specially close to the gods. Some temple carvings showed mothers of pharaohs standing next to a god as the pharaoh, her son, was created.

Courtiers and royal servants

Other women were close to the pharaoh in different ways. Women married to important nobles, who spent their lives at court, were often given titles such as Royal Ornament or King's Acquaintance. These reflected their position as the royal family's favourite and trusted friends. Women servants also spent their lives at the palace, looking after the needs of the royal family from the cradle to the grave. Some pharaohs brought concubines to live near the palace, in the royal ipet.

Three famous women rulers

Women, by tradition, could not be rulers of Egypt. Only a man could be a divine ruler – a living god – which is what the Egyptians believed their pharaohs to be. But some royal women found ways of exercising power and ruling Egypt.

HATSHEPSUT
(ruled 1473–1458 BC)

Hatshepsut was the daughter of a pharaoh and was married to Pharaoh Thutmose II, but they had no sons. When Thutmose II died she was appointed regent to his son (by another wife), Pharaoh Thutmose III. It was very unusual for a woman to be given such responsibility.

Keeping control

As regent, Hatshepsut was expected to hand over power to the new pharaoh as soon as he was old enough to rule. But she had herself crowned pharaoh, and became co-ruler with the young boy. Even after Thutmose III became an adult, Hatshepsut continued to rule Egypt. She was often shown on monuments dressed as a man and performing religious ceremonies normally carried out by male rulers. In writings, she was often referred to as king.

Queen Hatshepsut was often shown on monuments wearing a pharaoh's false beard and male clothing.

Successful ruler

Hatshepsut's army won many battles, and she sent trading expeditions to the rich kingdom of Punt (present-day Ethiopia). She probably stayed in power until she died. At her death, Thutmose III was crowned king. Many years later, her name was removed from her monuments, probably because people believed it was wrong for a woman to have had a pharaoh's power.

Queen Hatshepsut gave orders to build many fine buildings, including this temple at Deir el-Bahri. It is decorated with carvings showing the major events in her reign.

NEFERTITI
(1380–1340 BC)

Queen Nefertiti was the daughter of a senior palace official and wife of Pharaoh Akhenaten, who ruled from 1352 to 1336 BC. Nefertiti gave birth to six daughters, but there is no record that she ever had a son. Many carvings and paintings show the royal family as a close-knit group.

Power and influence

Nefertiti moved to live with Pharaoh Akhenaten at his new capital city at El-Amarna. In carvings she is often shown wearing a special crown, and standing by the side of the pharaoh as his equal. In one carving, she is in a war-chariot, fighting foreign enemies. Historians think this shows that Nefertiti had great influence over her husband. After 12 years Nefertiti seems to have disappeared from public life. She probably died just two years later. Her place was taken by her eldest daughter Meritaten.

Cleopatra VII (above right) was a skilful politician. She became famous for using her charm to win the help of powerful men.

CLEOPATRA VII
(ruled 51–30 BC)

Cleopatra was a member of a Greek ruling family who had governed Egypt since 305 BC. At first she co-ruled with her father (Ptolemy XII) and then with her brother (Ptolemy XIII). After a family quarrel Cleopatra lost power, but regained it with the help of Julius Caesar, the Roman general, who invaded Egypt in 48 BC. She began to rule with her second brother, Ptolemy XIV.

Defeat and death

In 48 BC Cleopatra gave birth to a son and claimed Caesar was his father. She gave orders for her brother to be killed and appointed her baby son as pharaoh. A few years later she married a Roman commander called Mark Antony, having given birth to his children (a twin boy and girl). In 34 BC Mark Antony gave Cleopatra the right to rule Egypt on behalf of Rome, but his enemies in Rome disapproved, and declared war. Mark Antony and Cleopatra were defeated in battle. They committed suicide, rather than be taken captive by Roman soldiers.

This carved and painted limestone portrait statue shows Queen Nefertiti wearing a dark-blue crown.

Palace fashions

Unlike ordinary working women, queens, princesses and upper-class women could afford fancy fashions. They wore fine wigs and wonderful jewels. These revealed the wearer's wealth and rank. The ancient Egyptians also believed that many items of jewellery, decorated with pictures of gods and animals, had magical, protective powers.

Long, straight styles

In the Old and Middle Kingdoms the favourite style for palace women was a long, slim linen dress reaching down to the ankles. In Egyptian art this kind of dress is usually shown with wide shoulder straps just above or just below the breasts (see page 19). However, no real-life examples of this style have been found. Surviving dresses usually have bodices and, sometimes, sleeves. These long, straight dresses looked elegant but would have been difficult to move in, and showed that the wearer did not have to do hard physical work.

Decorative beadwork

Egyptian dresses were almost always white because linen is difficult to dye. But palace women sometimes wore decorative open-work skirts or tunics, made of netting and glass or clay beads, over their dress. Bright turquoise blue was a favourite beadwork colour. Women also wore lacy openwork tunics made of fine leather.

This painting shows a woman from the New Kingdom era wearing a pleated dress in fine linen, with wing-like sleeves. She is also wearing a jewelled collar, headband and gold earrings and bracelets.

34

Fringes and pleats

By the New Kingdom, fashionable clothes had become looser and fuller, and were often decorated with fringes, or lots of crinkled pleats. There were several different pleating styles. No one is quite sure how these pleats were made, but it was probably either by pressing starched, damp clothes over ribbed wooden boards, or by twisting clothes very tightly when wet.

Wigs and tattoos

Wealthy women employed specially-trained servants, male and female, to cut and arrange their hair. Hairstyles changed over the years. In the Old Kingdom wealthy women wore their hair short. In the Middle Kingdom all women, rich and poor, grew their hair to shoulder-length, and wealthy women wore long, heavy wigs, sometimes decorated with beads and jewels. From about 1500 BC, many queens chose wigs in the Hathor style, named after the cow-goddess (see page 44). The wig had two front locks of hair wrapped round a disk-shaped weight. In the New Kingdom royal ladies often wore short, curly wigs, based on the haircut of Nubian soldiers, as well as wild, long ringlets. All women wore heavy make-up. Some royal women also decorated their skin with tattoos.

This carved stone relief is from the sarcophagus of Queen Kawit, who lived some time between 1560 and 1320 BC. It shows the queen seated on a chair holding a mirror and sipping a drink. A female servant is plaiting the queen's short, curly wig.

BEAUTY TREATMENT

For bald people, to make the hair grow: Take lion fat, hippopotamus fat, crocodile fat, cat fat, serpent fat and ibex (wild antelope) fat. Mix them all together and rub them on the bald areas.

To get rid of wrinkles on the face: Grind very finely: frankincense gum, wax, balanites oil and rush-nuts. Rub into the face every day.

A patterned glass vase shaped like a fish and made in about 1350 BC. It probably held scent. Egyptian women used oils and fats scented with natural resin (gum from plants) to scent and soften their skin.

WOMEN IN THE TEMPLE

Priestesses

Egyptian women played an important role in religion, as in many other areas of society. They might be priestesses, musicians or even wives of gods.

Servants of the gods

The Egyptians saw temples as the homes of the gods. They believed that worshipping in temples was a way of keeping order in the land of Egypt and in the universe. Priests and priestesses were both servants of the gods, and women could perform many duties. But priestesses usually held little authority and had to obey orders given by chief priests, who were men. Their most important task was to take care of the temples of the goddesses. (There were rarely priestesses for male gods.) They looked after the goddesses' statues, made offerings, and supervised temple servants and temple estates.

I have given to him [the god Amun] my daughter to be a god's wife and have endowed her better than those who were before her. Surely he will be gratified with her worship and protect the land of him who gave her to him.

CARVED STELE RECORDING HOW NITIQRET, ELDEST DAUGHTER OF PHARAOH PSAMTEK I (664–610 BC), BECAME A PRIESTESS

Limited powers

Because women could not read or write, priestesses never became 'lector priests' (senior temple staff who read out the prayers at each ceremony from a scroll). By the New Kingdom period, women had fewer duties in the temples. Most priests were men from the top ranks of society who had trained as religious scribes.

This Old Kingdom painting shows Princess Neferiabet, dressed as a priestess in a spotted panther skin. She is seated in front of a table, where offerings have been made to the gods. It was an honour for any woman to serve the gods and usually only princesses and noblewomen were chosen.

A stele carved with a portrait of the goddess Hathor. It is part of the temple built for Queen Hatshepsut (see page 32) in about 1470 BC.

Music for the gods

The Egyptians believed that music was an important way of communicating with the gods. Hathor, one of the chief female goddesses, was sometimes called Mistress of Music, and women singers, dancers and instrumentalists played a leading part in many temple ceremonies. While female choirs chanted or sang, women in temple orchestras played a jingling rattle, called a sistrum, tapped tambourines and other percussion instruments, and shook strings of beads. Unlike priestesses, women singers served in the temples of male gods as well as of goddesses. The name 'Singer of Amun' was an honourable title, given only to wives of senior scribes and nobles.

The god's wife

As part of their royal duties, many Egyptian royal wives became priestesses. The pharaoh himself was chief priest as well as ruler and army commander. In the Old Kingdom royal priestesses served the goddess Hathor. In later times they honoured other goddesses. From the New Kingdom onwards royal women, usually the pharaoh's daughter, might also become a wife of the chief male god, Amun. The title 'god's wife' was a very important one. A god's wife took part in special ceremonies to bring fertility and prosperity to the kingdom. She also controlled vast estates and had considerable political power. Weak pharaohs relied on the powerful priests of the god Amun, and on the 'god's wife', to help them rule.

A carved stone stele made in memory of a woman who served in the temple of the god Amun. She is shown (right), with her hands raised, praying to the seated god Osiris.

Worship and monuments

Temples were closely linked to the pharaoh and his government. Although ordinary men and women gathered in crowds outside temples on festival days, and prayed in temple courtyards to ask for special blessings, they never went inside. They were not allowed to set foot on a temple's holy ground because they were ritually impure. To meet their private religious needs, they worshipped in other ways, in village shrines and at home. If they could afford it, they paid for religious monuments to be built.

This painting from a private tomb in Thebes shows a noblewoman making an offering to the gods.

Family shrines

From the evidence of houses at Deir el-Medina, it seems that many women worshipped at small family shrines inside their own homes. Little statues, tables for offerings, stelae (stone slabs) and basins (dedicated to the goddess Tawaret) have all been found in workers' houses. Archaeologists think that these shrines were probably used mainly by women, who asked the gods and goddesses to protect their family's health and well-being by making offerings of food, drink and flowers.

Fertility figures

Women also prayed to the gods – especially to Hathor and Isis – to ask for children. Archaeologists have found many little dolls outside Hathor's temple in Dendera. They were probably fertility dolls, left there by women who were hoping to become pregnant. Women also left clay plaques, carved with the picture of the goddess Hathor, and special painted cloths outside Hathor's shrines. So far as we know, these cloths were never left by men.

A painted votive cloth, woven by women and showing women worshipping the goddess Hathor.

Statues and stelae

From the Middle Kingdom onwards, men were allowed to place statues in temple courtyards. These statues showed them making offerings to the gods, or praying. Women could not put up statues of their own, but might be included in their husband's or father's statue. Women were allowed to give stelae to stand outside temples. These were carved with family portraits and hieroglyphs praising a god or goddess, and mentioning the giver's name. Statues and stelae showed how important you were. The giver also hoped to win favour with the gods.

Second place or alone

Most stelae were given by men, because few women could afford them. Only rich noblewomen could afford expert carving in expensive stone. By tradition women took second place to men on funeral stelae. If they are pictured with a husband or son, they are shown as smaller. Sometimes they are shown alone, or with smaller, often female servants. Husbands and wives are never shown side by side, the same size.

My Majesty commissioned the work on it in Year 15, day 1 of the second month of winter... I did this for him [the god Amun] with affection, as a king does for a god. It was my wish to make it for him, gilded with electrum [silver and gold]... My mouth is effective in what it speaks: I do not go back on what I have said.

INSCRIPTION BY HATSHEPSUT, DESCRIBING TWO TALL OBELISKS IN HONOUR OF AMUN-RA [THE SUN-GOD] ORDERED BY HER FOR THE GREAT TEMPLE AT KARNAK

Two obelisks placed outside the temple of Amun at Karnak, one on the orders of Queen Hatshepsut, the other on the orders of her father Thutmose I.

DEATH AND BURIAL

Eternal life

Egyptian people believed that there was life after death. To them, death was just an interruption in a long process that stretched from birth to beyond the grave. To ensure eternal life, a dead person's body had to be properly preserved, and a dead person's friends or relations had to perform the correct rituals and make the right offerings at the tomb. Life after death was possible for women, just as much as for men. But men and women played different parts at funerals, just as they did in the rest of Egyptian life.

> When any important man dies, the women of the family smear their heads and sometimes their faces with mud. Then they walk through the city with their dresses tied up and their bosoms bare, hitting themselves as they walk along. All their women relations join in.
>
> REPORT BY HERODOTUS, A GREEK WRITER VISITING EGYPT (C.484–420 BC)

Part of a tomb-carving showing women taking part in a funeral procession. As part of their mourning, they are dancing and playing drums.

Arranging a funeral

Usually a dead person's son and heir would arrange their burial. Some ancient Egyptian wills state that only those children who helped with the funeral could inherit family property. But there were no laws forbidding women to organize funerals. If necessary women arranged for tombs to be prepared, bodies to be mummified, ceremonies to be held and funeral statues to be carved. Only rich families could afford elaborate mummies and beautifully-decorated tombs. Poor people had simpler burials. Rich or poor, women probably paid for funerals either out of their own wealth (from land, craft or trade) or by borrowing against property they hoped to inherit from the dead person.

The funeral ceremony of 'opening the mouth', from a papyrus made in about 1300 BC. There are women mourners crouching close to the mummified body of the dead man.

Ceremonies by men

Funeral ceremonies were conducted by special priests. In the Old Kingdom, women could be funeral priests, but this was no longer allowed in later years. But there are carvings and wall-paintings showing them making offerings and performing other rituals, and they may have continued to play an important part at burials. One of the most important ceremonies at a burial was called 'opening the mouth'. Its purpose was to allow the dead person's ka (spirit) and senses to return to the lifeless body, so it could live again. So far as we know, only male priests, or a son and heir, could perform this ceremony.

Professional mourners

Women played an important part in funerals as musicians and mourners. Tomb paintings often show women playing music close to the dead body. Tomb-paintings also show wives, daughters and crowds of other women weeping. Many families paid for groups of professional women mourners to walk in the funeral procession, weeping and tearing at their clothes and hair. These full-time mourners also danced and sang in honour of the goddess Hathor, who could help dead people be reborn in the next world.

Isis and Nepthys

Two women at each funeral represented the goddesses Isis and Nepthys, who were linked with death and rebirth. In myths they had searched for the murdered god Osiris, found his body, and restored him to life. By inviting Isis and Nepthys to the funeral, the dead person could also be helped to find new life.

A wall-painting showing a funeral procession on its way to the tomb. Men carrying a coffin and grave-goods (right), meet a group of women mourners (left)

Mummies and tombs

The New Kingdom scribe Ani, quoted right, was certain that men and women needed equal offerings after death, and deserved equal honour. But although women were buried with the same prayers and ceremonies as men, they were not given the same splendid grave-goods, and hardly any of them had their own individual tombs.

Mummies

Women's bodies, like men's, were mummified. The soft tissues were placed in four canopic jars, while the rest of the body was dried in natron (a natural salt), and wrapped in resin-soaked bandages. It was then sealed in a series of coffins, often decorated with portraits of the dead person, and symbols of gods, goddesses and lucky charms.

Shabtis

From the Middle Kingdom onwards little shabti figures were placed in the tomb, ready to do any work demanded of the dead person in the next world. All sorts of useful objects, from food and drink to stocks of fine linen and splendid jewels were buried there, to be used in the afterlife. From the New Kingdom onwards many tombs contained a copy of the Book of the Dead. This was a guide to the dangers of the afterlife, and how to survive them.

A mummy-case made for Princess Shepenmut, who died in about 700 BC. Although women were carefully preserved as mummies, they were buried in tombs belonging to their husbands or other family members.

This box contained shabti figures, made in about 1000 BC. It is decorated with a picture of a dead woman worshipping the goddess Nut, shown hiding in a sycamore tree.

Tombs were often decorated with carvings and paintings showing families reunited after death. These women and children from a powerful Egyptian family were portrayed in a tomb in about 2600 BC.

Not as rich as men

Even though men and women were buried in the same way, the goods left in tombs for men are much richer than those left for women. Maybe this reflects real life. Most Egyptian women were not as rich as men and depended upon their male relatives to provide beautiful objects and furnishings for them in death as in life.

Beautiful tombs

Rich Egyptians were buried in tombs cut deep into the ground. If they came from a very wealthy family, a tomb-chapel might be built at the entrance to the burial shaft. Prayers were said here, and offerings made, to satisfy the dead person's spirit, and to please the gods. Realistic statues (where the dead person's spirit could live) might be glimpsed through gaps in the tomb-chamber walls. Often a set of false doors marked the division between the world of the living and of the dead. Mourners and worshippers could not go through them into the tomb, but the dead person's spirit could come out, to receive offerings and hear prayers.

Second to men

These beautiful tombs show us that the Egyptians knew how to honour their dead. But almost all of them belong to men. And almost all the paintings, statues and carvings inside them show men at the centre of each scene, with women and girls in the background, or smaller, or to one side. As in life, men were more important as head of the family, while women usually played a secondary and supporting role. They were loved, valued and respected for their role in the family as mothers and home-makers, but were less important in the wider life of Egyptian society.

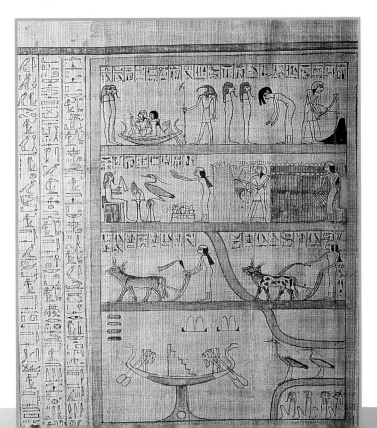

A painted papyrus showing Anhai, a princess from the Egyptian city of Thebes, who died in about 1150 BC. She is pictured enjoying eternal life in the next world.

GODDESSES

Ancient Egyptian gods and goddesses had many different powers. Worship did not depend on gender, and both men and women prayed and made offerings to goddesses and to gods. But by looking at some of the most important goddesses and their special powers, we can find out which female characteristics Egyptian people respected. For instance, most goddesses had powers to protect mothers and babies during pregnancy and childbirth. But sometimes goddesses were linked with events or skills that in the real world were associated only with men, such as warfare and writing.

Isis nursing her son by Osiris, the god Horus.

Hathor, the cow-goddess, was believed to have healing powers.

Isis
Isis was honoured by pharaohs as their mother. She was the heroine of a famous myth in which she searched for the dead body of her husband, the god Osiris, and restored him to life. She was worshipped as 'Isis great in magic', and was a cunning, skilful healer. She also protected young people and the sick. Isis was very popular, and was worshipped all over Egypt and the Mediterranean.

Nephthys
Nephthys was sister of the goddess Isis (above). She protected the dead.

Hathor
Hathor was known as the Cow-goddess. Like Isis she was worshipped as the mother of pharaohs. She was also the goddess of music and love. She shaped the future of newborn babies and protected the land of the dead in the west. She was specially honoured in the cities of Memphis and Dendera, where people built temples to her.

Neith
Neith was an ancient creator goddess, worshipped in the Nile Delta region. She was associated with warfare and crocodiles. People believed that she invented weaving, and associated her with mummy-making.

Nut

Nut, the sky-goddess, was mother of Isis and Nephthys. Every evening she swallowed the sun, and gave birth to it each morning. Her body was arched over the earth like the sky, and her robe was decorated with the stars.

Meshkent

Meshkent was the goddess of childbirth, shown as a female-headed brick. (Women sat on these during labour.) She also helped the dead to be reborn in the next world.

Maat

Maat, the goddess of truth and justice, was usually shown as a woman with an ostrich-feather headdress. She ruled the stars and the seasons, and kept good order throughout the universe.

Tawaret

Women prayed to Tawaret, the Hippopotamus-goddess, to protect them in childbirth.

Nekhbet

Nekhbet, the vulture-goddess, was a symbol of Upper Egypt. She was also a goddess of motherhood and birth.

Wadjyt

Wadjyt, the cobra-goddess, was a symbol of Lower Egypt. Like Nekhbet she protected pharaohs.

Tawaret

Renenutet

The cobra-goddess Renenutet protected pharaohs, and was a goddess of nursing, fertility and the harvest.

Serket

Serket, the scorpion-goddess, protected royal burials, and protected people against poison.

Seshat

Seshat was the goddess of writing and measurement, often shown as a woman dressed in a panther-skin. She helped pharaohs at the founding of new temples, and at other royal rituals.

Heket

The frog-goddess Heket protected women in childbirth, and shaped babies in the womb.

Bastet

The cat-headed goddess Bastet protected households. She was especially worshipped at New Year festivals.

Sekhmet

Sekhmet was a fierce lion-headed goddess of war, and daughter of the sun-god Ra.

Anat and Astarte

These foreign goddesses of war were introduced to Egypt in about 1500 BC from Syria and Palestine.

Bastet

GLOSSARY

afterlife The Egyptians believed that after they died their spirit would travel to the fields of happiness, so that they could enjoy life after death.

amulet A piece of jewellery that protects the wearer against danger and evil.

Amun The most important Egyptian male god.

archaeologist Someone who finds out about the past by investigating physical remains, such as objects and buildings.

barter To buy and sell by exchanging goods rather than money.

bias A one-sided view.

Book of the Dead A document that gave ancient Egyptians advice on how to avoid the dangers of death and reach the fields of happiness safely.

burial shaft A deep, narrow hole cut into the ground at the entrance to a tomb.

canopic jar A jar containing the inner organs removed from a dead body when the body was made into a mummy.

civilization A society with its own laws, customs, beliefs and artistic traditions.

concubine An unmarried woman living with a married man.

contract A legal agreement, usually written down in a special document.

courtier A nobleman or woman who lived and worked at the royal palace, helping to run the government, advising the ruler or offering friendship.

debts Something a person owes to someone else.

demotic One of the three styles of Egyptian writing, used for keeping business records.

domesticate To make an animal less wild, so that it can live alongside humans.

estate A large area of land, with houses, fields and farms, belonging to one family.

fertility doll A lucky charm shaped like a woman, buried in Egyptian tombs to help women and men have children in the afterlife.

grave-goods Clothes, jewels, books, furniture and other goods buried alongside a dead person for them to use in the afterlife.

guardian A person who is legally responsible for looking after someone else.

heir Someone who receives goods or land from a person who has died.

hieratic One of the three styles of Egyptian writing, used for religious texts.

hieroglyphs Picture-writing carved on temples and monuments. It is the oldest form of Egyptian writing.

household All the people, including family, servants and slaves, who live in one house.

impure Spiritually unclean.

inherit To pass on goods or land from one generation to another.

inscription Writing carved on stone.

interpretation An explanation of a piece of evidence, such as a picture or a document.

ipet A building where royal women lived.

memorial A building or work of art made to help people remember someone who has died.

midwife A woman trained to help mothers in childbirth.

monument A large building or statue put up in a public place.

mourner A person who shows sorrow and performs special rituals after someone's death.

mummified Preserved by being dried then wrapped in resin-soaked bandages.

mummy A dead body that has been mummified.

Nubia A country to the south of ancient Egypt, now part of the Sudan.

obelisk A tall stone pillar.

offerings Gifts offered to goddesses or gods.

ostracon (plural: ostraca) A small piece of stone or pottery with words or drawings scribbled on it.

overseer Someone who oversees people's work.

papyrus An early form of paper, made from reeds.

pharaoh The ruler of Egypt. The ancient Egyptians believed pharaohs were descended from the gods.

plaque A small piece of carving fixed to a wall.

profession A job involving a particular skill.

rank A person's position in society.

rebirth Being born again after death. The Egyptians believed that a dead person's spirit could be reborn.

regent Someone who governs on behalf of a child or a person who is unable to rule.

ritual A set way of performing a religious ceremony.

sarcophagus A container for a dead body, usually made from stone.

scribe A person trained to write documents and keep written records.

shabti A little figure, placed in a tomb to perform work in the afterlife on behalf of a dead person.

shrine The holiest part of a temple, where the statue of a god or goddess was kept.

stele (plural: stelae) A carved stone slab.

temple A big building where gods and goddesses were worshipped. The Egyptians believed that temples were homes for the gods.

thresh To separate grains of wheat or barley from their stalks.

tomb A place where a dead body is buried.

tribute Goods demanded by rulers from their people, and from conquered lands.

vizier A chief royal official.

votive cloth A piece of fabric made as an offering to goddesses or gods.

warp threads The threads stretched horizontally across a weaving loom.

wet-nurse A servant who breastfeeds another woman's baby.

will A document made by someone, giving instructions about what should happen to their property when they die.

workshop Building where people work and goods are made.

world of the dead The place where the ancient Egyptians believed dead people's spirits went after they died.

FURTHER READING (FOR OLDER READERS)

Stead, Miriam *Egyptian Life (*British Museum Press*)*

Dictionary of Ancient Egypt (British Museum Press)

Robins, Gay *Women in Ancient Egypt* (British Museum Press, 1993)

INDEX